Matt Cardle

My Story

Matt Cardle

My Story

THE OFFICIAL **X FACTOR** WINNER'S BOOK

Photography by Simon Harris

HarperCollins*Publishers*

Foreword by Dannii Minogue

I'll never forget the first time I ever heard Matt sing. I was utterly blown away by the beautiful tone of his voice and I knew he had so much potential. When I met him at Judges Homes in Australia he had trouble looking me in the eye during his performances. He had no ego, in fact I would say he was lacking in confidence of his ability to become a star. All it takes sometimes is one person to believe in you. That gives you the strength to make your dreams come true.

It's been amazing watching him grow week after week, both in confidence and in his performance. Many of my friends and fans of the show have told me how Matt has moved them to tears more than once, and that it's not only down to his incredible voice, but also the fact that he truly means every word he sings. Music is his number one love and passion.

Matt has been an absolute dream to work with and without a doubt one of the most popular contestants we've ever had with the crew, judges and other acts. He's a genuinely nice guy. He's friendly and polite to everyone and so grateful for all the help that everyone has given him on *The X Factor*.

I can't wait to see how things take off for Matt now. I have no doubt that he's going to be a huge star for years to come. He's so versatile that I can see him trying out all kinds of different musical styles in the future. I want to be in the front row of his first tour and I'll be waving the Team Minogue flag!

I want to say a big thank you to Matt for being such a dream to work with. He absolutely won't let you down!

Thanks for all your amazing support.

Love & Kisses

Dannii

XX

STARTING
OUT

In the beginning

I was contestant 219900, and I was just one of hundreds of thousands who decided to try out for this year's *The X Factor*. It was something I'd been mulling over for a few years, and this year I suddenly found myself standing among all these other people, clutching my number.

I was born Matthew Cardle on 15 April 1983 in Southampton. At that point I had one brother, Dominic. He's a year and a half older than me and we've always been close. In fact, my whole family are really close and get on very well. I had a nice, chilled-out childhood and a pretty normal upbringing.

I was a healthy baby, but when I was 18 months old my parents David and Jennifer discovered that I had a rare form of cancer called Wilms' tumour. I had a rash on my foot, and my mum, being a bit neurotic at the time, took me to hospital.

They did some tests, and I don't know the ins and outs of it but they found out I had a tumour on my kidney, which was pretty savage. I had to have chemotherapy, and all of my hair fell out. I then got something called adhesions, which is where scar tissue kind of messes up your insides. That ended up being more dangerous than the actual cancer, because I got blood poisoning and I spent a lot of time in hospital.

I was there for about a year in all and my parents must have absolutely hated it. It must have been horrendous for them, and when you think of how many people are going through similar things now ...

Luckily I made a full recovery and I've been fine ever since. In fact, if you have a kidney taken out at such a young age the other one grows to compensate, because it knows it's on its own, so you get one really powerful kidney, which is mad.

Apparently as a little child I used to make a lot of noise all the time. My folks always said I'd make a lot of racket but it would always be in tune. So I suppose I was already showing some kind of musical ability, no matter how clunky, and maybe that was setting me up for being a singer.

When I was really young we lived in Bristol and I used to go to a primary school there. Then when I was about five we moved to Essex and I went to the primary school at Stoke College in Suffolk. I stayed at Stoke until I did my GCSEs, so I was at the same school for around 12 years. I boarded there for a few months when I was doing my GCSEs. I wasn't doing my homework very well at home, so they thought it might be a good idea. It was only for a short time, but I loved boarding – it was something different for a while.

I messed about a lot at school and I was pretty annoying, to be honest. But I was bright as well, which is what wound up the teachers. I was more than capable of doing the work, but I was just a bit destructive and enjoyed having a laugh more than actually doing any of the stuff I should have been doing.

I was about six when I made my first career choice. I decided that I wanted to be a marine biologist, because I loved sharks. I still do actually, and I've always wanted to work with them in the Florida Keys or somewhere. That's still a bit of a dream of mine. But as I got older I realised that I was no good at biology, maths or physics, so that idea kind

opposite page

Me with my grandma as a toddler

of went out the window. I don't think being a marine biologist and being rubbish at biology go hand in hand.

When I was about nine or ten I started really getting into Nirvana and it gave me a proper taste for music. A year or so later, I picked up a guitar for the first time and that was it. I knew from that moment on that all I wanted to do was sing. That single moment changed my life for ever and I knew I could never go back. I guess it's like when you eat some really amazing food and you know you'll never feel satisfied unless you can eat that food again. For me, singing became like an addiction. It made me feel so good and gave me a real sense of direction even from that young age.

I had guitar lessons and also some singing lessons from the age of about 11, but then I missed a singing lesson and I was worried that the teacher would tell me off when I went back, so I missed the next one and then the next one, and I ended up not seeing her again. I stuck with the guitar, though, and as soon as I learnt enough chords I started writing my own songs. Looking back, I wouldn't say they were all amazing, but it was about getting experience and I think starting so young taught me a hell of a lot.

I began appearing in school productions and also joined bands at school – it was the only thing I really stuck at. My first band were called Chlorine, which was part of a Silverchair lyric, but looking back it was a terrible name for a band. I still love Silverchair, and Rage Against the Machine. But then, I also like Katy Perry, so I suppose my tastes are quite eclectic.

We were shocking as a band, I have to admit. I had long bleached hair and thought I was really cool and probably quite misunderstood. We used to play at a place called the Oliver Twist pub in Colchester quite a lot, but even though we were always practising and trying our best, I don't think we were ever going to change the face of music and eventually we split up.

I still stuck with music, though. I had this amazing music teacher called Adrian Marple, who is a legend and I'm still mates with him now. He

opposite

An early appearance on stage, in one of my bands

even came to see me at one of the live shows. Adrian always encouraged me a lot and we did all sorts of really unusual productions at school like *Sergeant Pepper* and *Tubular Bells*. They were a bit of a change from the usual *Guys and Dolls* and *Bugsy Malone*, and it was brilliant to get to do something different. We even got on *The Big Breakfast* when I was 13, because we were the first school ever to do a production of *The Wall*. It was a bit rubbish because all we did was play the show out for about 30 seconds, so it was kind of pointless us being there. Plus I'd wanted to meet Denise Van Outen, who was hosting it at the time, but that day Richard Bacon and Mel B's sister were presenting instead, so I was doubly disappointed.

I started singing lessons again when I was 13, and I also started going to the Lights, Music, Action! band camp, which was like a summer school. I ended up going every year bar one until I was 18 and it was wicked fun. It was one of those experiences I always look back on really fondly. It was held at Culford School, a massive private school in Suffolk. I was there for ten days and we got to choose if we wanted to do musical theatre or dance or be in a band. We'd learn the shows and mess about and have a laugh, and then at the end of it we'd put on shows for friends and parents.

I met two long-term girlfriends while I was there, and each time we started going out after singing the same song together. With both girls I duetted on 'Don't Give Up' by Peter Gabriel and Kate Bush, so in the end it became more of a pulling tool than a song.

The first girl was called Laura and I really fancied her. Adrian called me up just before summer school one year and told me she wanted to do a duet with me. I didn't believe him, but he basically set it up for me. We sang 'Don't Give Up', and afterwards we went out for about a year. I'm still grateful to him for that.

I missed the following year of band camp, but when I went back, this girl Hannah was there who I'd met two years previously. I said to Adrian, 'Oh my god, I think I'm in love with Hannah.' She was gorgeous, and a

model, so you can imagine. We also ended up duetting on 'Don't Give Up' and then I went out with her for two years. That song has definitely served me well.

After leaving school, I went on to do a music course at Colchester Institute, where Dermot O'Leary also went, funnily enough. But then one day I went out and bought a skateboard and I haven't put it down since. I spent the next two years at the skate park learning to skate and not going to any lectures, so needless to say I didn't do very well. Skating basically ruined that course for me.

I then went to Braintree College to do a media course, but as soon as I arrived they opened up Braintree Skate Park around the corner and I thought, 'What are you doing to me?' It felt like some kind of conspiracy. Sure enough, I ended up spending every day there and wasted another course through skating.

After that, I decided that maybe education wasn't for me, and for the next five or six years I ended up playing in bands, skating and taking on all sorts of jobs so I could pay for studio time.

I've had so many jobs along the way I've lost count. I worked in a wood factory making furniture, in a plastics factory and as a bricklayer. I was doing industrial flooring for three years, I drove around the country for a year trying to sell advertising space, and I did garden maintenance. I also worked as a postman, a milkman, in fast-food restaurants, in coffee shops and bars, and one year I was even Santa. I was only 18 and I had these little Reebok Classics sticking out the bottom of the outfit. I looked absolutely ridiculous and, as you can imagine, my heart wasn't in it. Probably the weirdest job I've ever had was working for the Great British Circus, putting up and taking down cages for lions on a film set. I also put posters up for the circus, advertising that they were coming to perform.

I could go on and on – that's probably only about half the jobs I've done – but they were basically a means to an end and I'm not sure I ever enjoyed any of them. The only way I was getting through them was by thinking of the money. I was always putting off getting a real job because I knew all I wanted to do was sing, and I thought that if I settled down and got a proper, sensible career it would have been like admitting I hadn't made it as a singer, and I just didn't want to believe that was the case. The longer I could go on doing jobs here and there and not caring about them, the longer I could convince myself I was doing the right thing by waiting for a break.

My main job over the years – or rather, the one I've done on and off for the longest – has been painting and decorating. I've never made any secret of the fact that I'm a bit of a bum, and it's not something I'm ashamed of because I always had it in the back of my mind that I was going to make more of myself one day. I was doing decorating work simply because it was easy and I could do it, but I found it monotonous and I hated every minute of it. I made sure I kept my life away from work interesting by singing and seeing my mates. And that brings us back round to *The X Factor*.

this page

After all my time playing in bands, it was great to get the opportunity to take my guitar on *The X Factor* stage

I knew that entering it could mean the end of magnolia all over my face and hands. The end of paintbrushes, the end of decorating hotel rooms. It was potentially the break I needed, which is why I turned up that day back in June, even though I was definitely in two minds about it for a while. Mainly because I was already in another band.

I've been in a couple of bands since leaving school. The first one was called Darwyn, and we all met at the last band camp I did. I had a handful of songs I'd written that I rated and I showed them to my now best mate Alistair McMillan, who is a drummer and percussionist, and two other guys, one called Duncan, also a drummer, and Richard, who is a pianist. They were like 'Wow, these songs are cool, let's make a band.' So, er, we did.

Duncan was going to be the drummer and Ali the percussionist, but Ali was the better drummer so it didn't really work out that well at first. We had some rehearsals at Richard's house and when Duncan didn't turn up one day, Ali jumped on the drums and it worked out really well, so that became the band – the three of us.

We were together for almost three years and we slogged it out locally and around London, gigging wherever we could. We were constantly travelling. We had a tiny little Volkswagen Caddy and I was always the one sitting on this seat in the back that we'd pulled out of an old Ford Cortina. Every time we went around a corner I'd get Ali's drums falling on my face or Richard's piano collapsing on me. It was all properly basic but it was the most fun time. Driving to a gig with your best mates, talking rubbish and getting excited about performing, is the best thing. I absolutely loved it.

It was funny because we never actually split up as a band, we just kind of stopped one day. No one was listening to us much – which was a shame because we were really good – so we started to lose interest. We recorded an album while we were together, but deep down we knew that the album was never going to go anywhere because we produced it ourselves so it wasn't exactly amazing. We weren't signed or anything, so we put it together using money my granddad gave us.

this page

My first audition

Also, Richard's mum is a Spitfire pilot and she was teaching him to fly, so when he got trained up fully he started doing displays and he wasn't as interested in rehearsing as Ali and I were. When you've spent the day flying up the Thames Estuary in a Spitfire you don't really want to go and hang out and rehearse.

I think the basic problem was that we were in the wrong place at the wrong time. We were in this tiny village working our arses off in this little acoustic rock band, and it just didn't happen for us.

We all stayed friends after the band ended, though, and in September 2010 Ali and I went back to one of our old haunts – the Five Bells pub in Colne Engaine, Essex – to perform, and it was nice to revisit it all. It was filmed for *The X Factor* and I don't think the locals knew what to make of it, but it was such a brilliant night.

Even after Darwyn faded out, I was still writing songs constantly, so I had another half an album's worth of songs. I was 24 at the time and keen to get into another band. My friend Neillo's band had just split up, so he suggested we make a new band. He introduced me to a couple of guys called John Holland and Alex Baker, who played drums and bass, and it all kind of kicked off from there.

We called ourselves Seven Summers, and even though the first couple of rehearsals were a bit disastrous, things suddenly clicked and we started playing really well together. Back in January 2010 we released a self-titled album, and amazingly after my first few live shows on *The X Factor* it went in at number 26 on the Amazon download chart. That gave me a great feeling. To think of the other lads doing well and also benefiting from me being on the show made me really happy, because I had the time of my life in that band. We played quite a lot of gigs and I've got such good memories of us being together.

'There's nothing like the buzz of being that close to people when you're performing.'

I do miss playing the small venues I used to do sometimes. I've always wanted to play on a big stage and have a big audience, but with the pubs and clubs it's way more relaxed and if you mess up a song or forget the lyrics it's not the end of the world. If you mess up in front of 17 million people it's pretty bad, so there's a lot more pressure.

I would love to do some more pub gigs when I get a chance. I'd like to do some really nice intimate gigs where my friends and family and fans can come along. There's nothing like the buzz of being that close to people when you're performing. The whole atmosphere is different and you can kind of lose yourself.

The all-important audition

I had thought about auditioning for *The X Factor in* 2010, but because Seven Summers was going really well I'd decided to leave it for another year and see how things went. But then my ex-girlfriend Lauren's friend Jurga filmed me in a pub and sent the video in to *The X Factor*.

Following my application for the show, I got a call asking me to go along for the live auditions and of course it was an amazing opportunity, but I was honestly still in two minds about going. In the end I decided that I wanted to see what Cheryl looked like in the flesh, and also to hear what Simon had to say about my voice. I love doing things under pressure, because it's such a good learning experience, so I thought, why not? The worst that could happen was that I'd get sent home with a no, and at that point I wasn't thinking or worrying about that.

I chose four songs to take along to perform for my audition – all girls' songs, funnily enough. I picked Lady GaGa's 'Paparazzi', Amy Winehouse's 'I'm No Good', Duffy's 'Mercy' and 'Jolene' by Dolly Parton. I wanted songs that I already knew like the back of my hand because I didn't want to mess up. Ali and I used to go and perform at pubs and clubs together as a duo sometimes, and I used to sing those tracks and knew them really well, so it made sense.

My dad drove me to the audition at the ExCel Centre in London because he was flying to Russia from City Airport, which is right nearby. So I walked over from there and joined the queue. I was there for about four hours before I got to sing for the judges, and for about seven hours afterwards. Because I got good feedback from the judges, ITV wanted me to hang around so they could film me some more. It was a long day but a really good one, although it seems so long ago now.

I'm not going to lie, I was absolutely petrified when it was time for me to go up on stage and audition for the judges. I was wondering why I'd even gone along. It was completely insane standing in front of Louis, Cheryl and Simon.

I remember saying to the judges, 'I'm here to do my level best and just see what I can or can't do,' but everything from then on felt quite unreal. Being on stage singing was a bit of a blur. It was weird hearing my voice coming out over a sound system and thinking, 'Simon Cowell can hear that too.' And then there were the 3,000-odd other people looking at me too.

I was concentrating so hard on not forgetting my words and I felt really tense, but then about half-way through 'I'm No Good' I started to relax a bit and even enjoyed some of it. I was aware I was looking at the floor a lot, but that was because it was less scary than looking up and seeing everyone watching me.

When I finished, the crowd gave me a great reaction, and I could see that the judges were smiling – though that isn't always a good thing. It was only when Louis said, 'You've got a very unusual voice. It's a great voice and you're very musical,' that I felt a tiny bit more relaxed. He also said I was awkward and quirky, both of which are probably true, but thankfully he said, rather than thinking I was a bit weird, he liked those things about me.

Getting a yes from Cheryl was incredible. But of course I still had to get Simon's verdict, which is always the tough one. I was fully expecting him to tell me I was dreadful or something, because I was so desperate for him to like my performance, so when he said something along the lines of 'I really like you, so you're going to get a big yes from me as well' I felt as though my legs were going to give way. I don't think I've ever felt that happy in my life.

Walking off the stage and seeing my friends and Dermot backstage was also bizarre. It all felt like it was happening to someone else. I remember Dermot asking me how I was feeling, and I said that all I wanted was a beer and a fag, and it was true. I needed to sit down and take in everything that had just happened and try and make it feel real.

I phoned my dad to say I'd got through to Bootcamp. He was really pleased, and then the next night I went out to celebrate with my mates.

this page

Filming on set at Bootcamp

A lot of them didn't even know I'd been for the audition, so they were shocked when I told them I was on my way to Bootcamp. I remember telling the other members of Seven Summers that I'd got through to Bootcamp, but I said that once it was over we'd just get on with the band, because I honestly didn't think I'd reach the next stage, so we'd just carry on as we were before. I never saw *The X Factor* as the end for us.

I had some time off before Bootcamp started, and I spent 99.9 per cent of it at the skate park. I've never stopped skateboarding. I was still going out with my mates, and also finishing off some painting in a hotel, so it's not like anything else in my life changed. This was work I'd agreed to do, and I was trying to get it all done and dusted in time for Bootcamp, as I had no idea what would happen from then on. It might be just a bit of short-term fun or it could be the start of something big.

Bootcamp and beyond ...

After a few weeks of waiting, on 22 July it was time for us to go to Wembley Arena in London for Bootcamp. This was another step closer to the live finals and I couldn't wait to perform again. But on the flip side I knew that if I did a rubbish job it would mean the end of *The X Factor* for me. In those weeks following the audition I'd started to think that maybe I could do well in the competition, and even to see beyond Bootcamp and what doing well could mean. I knew I never wanted to go back to painting, whatever happened.

My mate Billy gave me a lift to Wembley Arena, but once we were there I didn't want to get out of the car. I'd had a couple of drinks the night before, which wasn't a clever idea, and I wasn't feeling great. Then I saw all these people turning up and going in and I wanted Billy to turn the car around and take me back to Essex.

Sitting in the car outside the Arena, I had that awful first-day-of-school feeling and I didn't know if I could go through with it. Then one

of the girl bands turned up and they looked amazing and I turned to Billy and said, 'I'm feeling better now, thanks for the lift, see you later,' and I got out of the car.

Once I was inside with everyone else I looked around and saw around 200 other people who all looked as if they belonged on *The X Factor* – and I just didn't look like them. I had a beard and a funny hat, a checked shirt and a sore head. I didn't look or feel like an *X Factor* contestant. I wondered if other people were looking at me and thinking the same, but for whatever reason, I'd got there and I had to give it a go. It was a really weird time, because I was still feeling like Seven Summers were going to stay together, but I felt totally torn because something in me wanted to give all of this a good go as well.

All of the contestants were put up in a hotel nearby and I had to share a room with a stranger, which was a bit odd. He was a guy called Carl who was nice enough but we didn't exactly bond or anything. There were all these rumours of wild parties at the hotel, but if they were going on I certainly didn't take part in any of them. I know things got a bit crazy one night because there was a lot of noise, but I spent most of my time in the room chilling. I quite like getting away from it all and having time on my own, so I took the chance when I could, because the days were pretty manic and you didn't really get a second to yourself.

Cheryl was still recovering from illness and Dannii was on maternity leave in Australia during Bootcamp, so it was Simon and Louis who were deciding our fate. I don't think there was one person there who wasn't feeling absolutely terrified. It's all very well getting good comments during the auditions, but you're up against over 200 other acts who have also had good feedback, and everyone has been put through for a good reason.

When we were all standing on the stage on the first day, Louis gave us a pep talk which was something along the lines of 'Bootcamp is tough. Showbusiness is tough. You've got to be tough. You've got to go out there and deliver.' Then Simon basically told us that one of us was going to win *The X Factor*, and that we had a hell of a lot to prove. He also told

us that doing well in the competition would change our lives for ever. I remember thinking, 'Great, no pressure then.'

We already knew that half of the acts that were there would be sent home the next day, so we all had a lot riding on that first performance. We were split into four categories – girls, boys, over-25s and groups – and each category was given a song to sing. I was in the over-25s, and our first challenge was to make our own version of Lady GaGa's 'Poker Face'. I'm a massive fan so it was great for me and I was really pleased.

The judges' thinking was that if we all sang the same song they could judge us purely on our vocal talents and how we could put a bit of a spin on a song, which made a lot of sense. They needed to see early on if we were right for the competition or not, so they wanted to see who stood out. The verse is quite monotone, so I made a nice melody out of it to make it a bit different.

I thought my performance went pretty well, but then we had to wait until the following day to see if we'd made it or not. We were divided into groups, and I could tell that everyone was looking around to see who else was in their group, trying to gauge whether or not they were being sent home or kept in. I saw a few people in my group who I had thought were really good, so I felt hopeful, but I knew that nothing was guaranteed and this could be the end of the whole thing for me. I felt bad thinking about having to get my bag and go back home and tell everyone I hadn't made it.

Eventually the judges broke the news about who was coming back the next day, and when I found out I was one of them I was totally overwhelmed. I was also really shocked, because some of the acts I'd really rated had been sent home. Of course I was well chuffed to still be there, but it made me realise it was pretty cut-throat.

Because there were so many people, there was quite a lot of waiting around, so I found myself eating and lying around a lot. There were a few moments when I looked around and people would be getting together in groups and doing *Glee*-style singing and I was like, 'I do not belong here.'

But I wasn't the only one who felt that way, and the more I spoke to other contestants the more I realised that. As I was with the over-25s, for a lot of the time I was hanging out with Mary and John, who were both lovely.

We were up bright and early the next morning, and back at Wembley Arena we found out that we were doing a dance masterclass with Brian Friedman. I think a lot of people really surprised themselves that day, and a lot of people who didn't think they would, quite enjoyed it, apart from Zayn from One Direction who decided he didn't want to do it and did a runner, which I found hilarious.

The masterclass was one of those moments in life when you have to shake off any inhibitions and think, 'You know what? There are a lot of people watching me do this but I don't care.' It ended up being great and I really enjoyed it. I don't think Justin Timberlake will be quaking in his boots about my dancing skills, but it was a laugh, and I felt like at least I gave it a go. That's all you can do really, isn't it? I gave it everything I had.

Before we headed back to the hotel, Louis told us we were being given a list of 40 songs, and we had to choose one to sing the following day. The minute I looked down at the sheet of paper I saw that Roberta Flack's 'The First Time (Ever I Saw Your Face)' was on the list. I'd sung it at my surrogate brother's wedding, so I immediately called him up and I was like, 'Jules, you will not believe what's on the list.' I knew I had to sing it.

It's a song that means so much to me. It was dedicated to my mum's best friend, Sharon, who died in a car crash 16 years ago when I was 11. She left behind her four sons, Julian, 17, Ben, 11, and the twins Rob and Tom, eight. The eldest son, Jules, phoned up my mum and said he didn't know what they were going to do now Sharon had gone. Mum immediately said to him, 'Well you're mine now. Come to the house.' Their dad was around but things weren't so good, so when the other boys weren't at boarding school they were round at ours most of the time as well, so our family grew overnight, which was great.

My mum took on those kids and they literally made our family bigger and better. All of their school photos are mixed up with mine on

the wall and we're all so close. They were always down at the live shows and I'm planning to move in with Tom next year.

Jules met his wife under very sad circumstances too. They worked in the same office, and one day she was crying in the corridor. He went over to see if she was alright and she said, 'Look, you wouldn't understand.' He was like, 'Try me,' and then she told him her mum had just died of cancer. He said he knew how she felt and talked to her about what happened with his mum. They kind of looked after each other from then on, and they ended up getting married.

I sang that song 'The First Time' at their wedding as she came into the church. The whole day was one of the most emotional of my life and one that will stay with me for ever.

When the final day of Bootcamp came, for some reason I was absolutely ready for it. All of a sudden I felt alert and ready to fight for my place. I was still really nervous but I was happy with the song I was singing, even though I wasn't sure what the judges would make of it.

When Simon announced that Nicole Scherzinger was joining us, it kind of brought everything up a notch, because there was someone else to impress. She joked that it was time to separate the men from the boys and the pussycats from the dolls, which I liked.

I had to wait quite a while for my audition, which gave me far too much thinking time, and it made me realise that the closer you get to something, the more you want it. It's like when you start your driving lessons: you don't mind the idea of failing the test until you've been in a car and driven it around. It felt a bit like that, but way more important.

I'd taken a bit of a risk with the song I'd chosen because it was a girl's song, and I was the only guy in Bootcamp doing that song. I thought it was right to take a risk at that point, just to stand out. But I started to get more and more nervous, because if I'd gone out there and hadn't nailed it, then I'd know I should have done better.

It didn't help that we were all watching each other perform, because so many people were really talented and everyone had upped their game.

opposite page

Taking a moment backstage before my next performance

Every time someone else did a killer performance I thought, 'That's it, they've got my place. I'll never be as good as them.' It was horrible. I actually refused to watch anyone right before my audition, because I knew it would make me even more nervous, so I spent most of my time pacing up and down the corridors on my own.

I was petrified when my name was called and I had to go up on stage. I remember telling the judges how lucky I felt to be there, surrounded by such talented people, and also saying that I hoped they thought I was a potential star. It may have seemed a bit cheesy, but it was how I was feeling at the time.

Singing 'The First Time' again made me feel incredibly emotional, to the point where I started crying half-way through. Thankfully I managed to hide it and I didn't mess up, but I welled up and had to blow it out. I did have a proper cry afterwards, though, when I was on my own.

Before we went home at the end of that day, Simon pointed out that of the 200,000 people who auditioned for *The X Factor*, we were the final 100. It was then that it finally hit home how real everything was. I think in some ways I was still drifting along feeling like everything was a bit of a dream, but now it was game on. Every single one of us had a genuine chance of winning the show, which was insane.

I was really pleased with how my performance went and obviously I meant every word that I sang, but I was conscious afterwards that I maybe didn't make eye contact enough, so I was a bit annoyed at myself. I said to Dermot that I prayed I'd done enough, and I meant it. Nobody wanted to go home, and the last thing I wanted to do was to go back to living with my parents and painting walls. There was a golden opportunity right there in front of me and I wanted to grab it with both hands and never let it go. It was a big risk but it paid off, and I honestly think that's the moment that got me to the live show.

The next few hours were going to determine which path my life was going to take, and god did they drag. The judges had a tough job

opposite page

Backstage with
Nicolo and Aiden

deciding who should stay and who should go, but I wasn't thinking about that. All I could think was 'Put me out of my misery. Tell me one way or the other.'

We were all called back on stage and Simon told us that there had been some changes to the competition. The first was that the over-25 age limit had been raised to 28, which meant that I was now in the boys' category. At first it was a bit of a shock and I was really worried about it, but the more I thought about it the more I realised it would be a positive thing for me to be in the younger category. I don't consider myself to be a man – I'm still a little kid at heart – and I guess it suited me better. I was desperate not to come across as too old in the competition anyway, so it worked out really well.

The second bit of news was that instead of taking six acts from each group through to Judges' Houses, they were taking eight. This was brilliant news. I was still up against a hell of a lot of competition, but it meant that my chances of being chosen had suddenly improved slightly, so if I had been just outside their original six I could now be in with a chance of bagging one of the other two places.

When my name was called out I was completely gobsmacked. It was partly about the fact that it was Nicole who had said my name. In my head I was going, 'Nicole Scherzinger just said my name.' I was just so happy and I got really emotional. I immediately started thinking about where we'd be going, who our mentor could be, all of that stuff. So much was going through my head.

Again it was my dad I phoned to say I'd made it, and then I called Jules, Tom, Rob and Dom and I was like, 'You're not going to believe it, I'm in the last eight.'

I felt so honoured to be in the competition with seven other amazing guys. I was over the frikkin' moon. Then when I later got put in the boys' category I got to know some of them, and got on really well with a guy called Aiden Grimshaw. Some of you may have heard of him? We got on from the word go and stayed really good friends throughout the competition.

We first spoke after I saw his performance of David Gray's 'This Year's Love'. I was like, 'Oh my god, that kid's got to get through, he's incredible.' I went and spoke to him afterwards and said I thought he was amazing, and he said the same to me. Then we both got through and that's when the bromance started!

After that, it was back home to reality, because I had to finish off all the painting I had booked in before I went to Judges' Houses. As I painted the last wall I thought, 'I never, ever want to do this again as long as I live.' Now all I had to do was get through Judges' Houses.

THE X FACTOR
DREAM

Judges' houses

It felt absolutely insane that I'd made it through to Judges' Houses. When we got to the airport and I found out us boys were going to Australia, I freaked. I mean, of all the places to get to go – Australia. I was hoping we'd go abroad somewhere because I've watched previous series and they've travelled to LA and Spain and places, but this was something else. I was in total shock. All my life I'd wanted to go to Australia, it's one of the places I'd always planned to visit.

As soon as we found out where we were going, of course we all guessed we were getting Dannii as our mentor, and I was so happy about that. When we got out there and found out Natalie Imbruglia was the guest judge, that was awesome too, because she's amazing.

I'd love to say I was excited about all aspects of travelling to the other side of the world, but I absolutely hate flying so I wasn't feeling great about the flight. I looked at the plane while we were waiting in the departure lounge and it was massive, so I was hoping it meant the journey would be less bumpy than the ones on the small ones I'd been on before. In any case, I wasn't about to let my fear of flying get in the way

opposite page

I felt like my whole life was about to change

of anything. I was going to Australia whatever happened. Nothing was going to stop me.

I was pretty terrified but before long the excitement of it all took over. One minute, *The X Factor* camera crew were interviewing me about how scared I was of flying, and then the next time they filmed me I was saying, 'I'm fine, it's all fine! Flying is fine!'

Before reaching Sydney we stayed in a really nice hotel resort in Port Douglas, where I shared a room with Karl Brown, who is a good guy. Then we were on the move again.

I fell in love with Sydney as soon as I got there. We had some downtime before our auditions and we got to do so many amazing things. We went jet skiing and to the beach, and the local zoo brought animals up to the villa. I held a koala that absolutely stank. I've never smelt anything so bad in my life. We went to see the Opera House and the Harbour Bridge, and I also managed to sneak out and see a friend of mine for some drinks at the Harbour Bar.

When we got to Judges' Houses I wanted so much to get through to the live finals. You get a lot of TV exposure during Judges' Houses and if you don't get through you'll always be known as that guy who didn't make it, and I was worried about how that would affect things I tried to do in the future.

All of us guys got on really well, and Aiden and I hung out together a lot, but the more time we spent out there, the more competitive it got between the eight of us. We knew that only three of us were going through, so things did get increasingly tense.

Waiting to do my performance was nerve-wracking. I got myself so wound up. I knew doing well that day could mean the end of having rubbish jobs and no direction. It could potentially turn my life inside out and upside down, which is what I wanted. So to have everything pinned on that one moment was scary.

The first song I did was 'Come Home' by OneRepublic. I basically stared at the floor for two minutes and then looked up briefly at the end.

All of us were warned by someone working on the show that Dannii and Natalie weren't happy that no one was looking at them, so I made sure I looked up for at least a bit of my second performance, of Beyoncé's 'If I Were a Boy'.

I found the auditions pretty tough. It's so hard when you're standing there with just a piano and you've got 30 production staff watching every move you make. I tried not to rush it, but I was keen to get it over as quickly as I could. Afterwards, I felt kind of okay, though I knew there were a couple of notes I could have hit a bit sharper.

When all of us had sung, Natalie and Dannii got together to discuss who they were taking through. It was a really weird feeling knowing that they were deciding our fate, but there was nothing left for us to do. There were no second chances – we couldn't storm in and demand to have another go. It was just a waiting game. It was indescribable how much of a difference a yes could make to me. It was either home time or it was game on. I'd been trying for so long and I'd been singing for so long, but that was just in sticky-floored pubs and this was all so different.

A big part of me believed that I could do it, but there was also a nagging voice that said, 'Why would you make it over anyone else? What makes you so special?' But at that moment, getting through to the live finals was so close.

All of us boys were standing on a veranda at the back of the villa, waiting for our names to be called so we could find out if we were through or not. When each person went off, they played loud music so the rest of us couldn't hear their reaction. Obviously they'd either be screaming or crying, which would be a dead giveaway.

When it was my turn, I really wanted to get it over with, but Dannii told me very slowly and painfully. She was talking with the saddest face. It was a beautiful face, of course, because it's Dannii Minogue, but she didn't look happy. She said some positive things, then some negative things, and then some more positive things. Then she held my hand and

kind of pulled me in and said, 'But I've made my decision now and I can't change it.' I was looking into her eyes thinking, 'Oh my god, you're not going put me through.'

Then, just as she was about to tell me the result, a plane flew overhead so she had to start all over again. Everyone was having a right laugh about it, but all I was thinking was 'This is my future we're talking about here.'

When Dannii eventually gave me a yes I was so spun out. I don't feel like I thanked her enough at the time, but that was because I couldn't get my head around it. Normality just goes out of the window when someone tells you something like that.

'I knew at that moment, more than ever, that I had to work harder than I'd ever worked before.'

My life had already changed so much, and now I was about to appear on live TV in front of millions of people. It had already been weird being recognised out and about; it's insane how five minutes on the telly can change everything for you.

I still just felt like me – even though I was sitting in Australia with Dannii Minogue and I'd just got through to the live shows, I didn't feel any different. I don't know how I thought I was going to feel. It's not like all of a sudden you become or feel famous. You feel exactly the same, but people know who you are. It's so surreal and the whole thing was a massive, massive gift. I knew at that moment, more than ever, that I had to work harder than I'd ever worked before. If I wanted to go all the way and make the live final I needed to have confidence that I deserved to be there, which meant putting everything I had into the coming weeks.

opposite page

Living out of a
rucksack, but loving it

The first person I called with the good news was my dad. The camera crew videoed it, and they asked me not to swear when I told him. I called him and said, 'It's bad news, I didn't get through,' and he started shouting bad language really loudly. Then, when I told him I was joking and that I was in the final three, he started shouting even more. He was really loud and I was like, 'Dad, Dad, you can't swear, this may be on TV.'

The next person I called to tell that I'd made it through was Neil from Seven Summers. Before I'd flown out to Australia, everything had seemed up in the air and we'd been making plans for when I got back, so I felt terrible telling him I wouldn't be around for a while, but he was cool about it.

At that point I didn't even know who else had got through, so I went back and asked one of the ladies who was working on the show. I was like, 'Tell me it's Aiden, please tell me it's Aiden.' When she said he'd made it I went and gave him the biggest hug I'd ever given anyone in my life.

We'd kind of mooted the idea of both of us getting through but had no idea what the chances were of it actually happening, so it was a brilliant moment. We were both so happy. We were a bit surprised about Nicolo, but we were really happy for him and it was an amazing moment when we realised we would all be moving in together.

I'd had a lot of people tell me to give up singing over the years, so I had many people to prove something to, and that day was the start of it all. Even though, at the end of the day, I was only doing it for myself, I'd be lying if I said it isn't a nice feeling to know that I'd done the right thing in carrying on for so long. People kept saying I needed to give up and get a job. You don't have to listen to those people, but you can't help hearing them; it's a bit depressing. Don't get me wrong, a lot of people were supportive – especially my family – but there are always those who want to put you down and label you a dreamer.

Before *The X Factor*, despite being in Seven Summers, I was feeling a bit desperate and upset about things. I still wasn't ready to give up, but I was thinking about going to another country, maybe a place where the music industry isn't as big as in the UK, so that I'd have more chance of getting noticed. I thought about going to live in China, or in Norway, where my cousins live, and try to make it over there. I was just throwing ideas around, and then *The X Factor* came along and saved me.

Getting a yes from Dannii felt great. I didn't even mind the flight back home too much – probably because I was on such a high. I had to psyche myself up again to get through it, but I was so excited about seeing my friends and family and celebrating that I didn't give it too much thought.

As soon as I got back to England, I went on a big night out in Shoreditch with my surrogate brothers. I wasn't allowed to tell anyone I had got through, so I was quietly happy that night. It was a great night.

this page

Suited and booted and ready for live TV

Going live

I had two weeks back at home with my family before the live shows started, and once again I spent the entire time skateboarding. Can you see a theme here? I knew I probably wouldn't get a chance to skate again for a while, so I decided to take full advantage of the time off and do as much as I could.

I still had some painting to finish off, but that was the last thing I could think about doing, so I got someone else to do it for me. I did do a few little live gigs, but word had got out that I was through to *The X Factor* live shows, so quite a lot of people turned up and things got a bit out of control, which was wicked.

I didn't worry too much about moving into the contestants' house. I just packed my bag and went with an open mind. Fashion isn't my thing,

so I didn't worry too much about what I was taking – just checked shirts, jeans, boots and a hat. That was me done.

I knew I'd miss my dog Stella a lot from the word go, and I was sad not to have her around. She's a black Labrador and is absolutely amazing. Obviously I'd get to see my friends and family when they came down to the show, but it was a bit different where she was concerned.

The contestants' house was stunning. It was also quite a weird experience stepping through the door on the first day because everyone was excited, on a real high, and people were kind of running around madly. I was sharing a room with Aiden and Nicolo, but Nicolo soon moved out because of my snoring. He didn't moan or anything, he just quietly left one day, bless him.

Having the wild cards come into the house in Week 1 was quite strange. For the most part I was really pleased, because TreyC, Paije and Diva Fever came back, but I never really understood why Wagner was brought back. But I suppose everyone deserves their chance and he did make great TV.

I didn't mind being in the house with everyone else at all. I was still living with my parents up until the show, so I was used to people being around. The house could be pretty manic, though, and Aiden and I kind of kept ourselves to ourselves most of the time. We either stayed in our room or played table tennis. Or if I wanted a bit of time to myself I'd listen to my iPod, watch *The Inbetweeners* or phone my friends.

Food in the house was usually takeaways because no one really bothered to cook. We weren't in the house a lot over the following weeks anyway, as we were often out rehearsing or doing shoots or interviews. It wasn't like we spent loads of nights lying in front of the TV or anything.

Things were full-on from the first day we moved into the house as we had to get everything sorted out for the live show. The first week went at a fairly slow pace compared to the later weeks, but there was still a lot to do. I was expecting it to be a busy time, but nothing could have prepared me for how frantic things actually became. It was all good though. I learnt a lot very quickly.

Week 1

It seemed to take forever for 9 October, the day of the first live show, to arrive. In some ways I was willing it to come quicker, but I was also so nervous that I was wondering how I was going to get through the evening.

Everything in the run-up was awesome. We had styling, both hair and make-up. The make-up was a bit interesting because it was the first time I'd ever worn it – honest. But there's something quite nice about having a brush rubbed over your face and I got used to it surprisingly quickly.

I've been cutting my own hair for about ten years, so having someone else touching it was a bit weird at first, but the hair stylist Adam Reed was amazing and in the makeover he gave me what he described as 'Something a little bit more stylised. We've got a bit of a Jude Law thing going on here.'

Considering I spend most of my time wearing a hat, I've never been that fussed about my hair. A lot has been made of my hat, but before the show I'd never even given it a second thought. I put it on and I take it off. I started wearing it a few years ago and all of a sudden it's become a big thing. I should have thought about it really, as everyone makes a big thing out of Dappy from N-Dubz's hat, but I suppose that's the power of telly.

I've been sent loads more hats since appearing on the show, but I only ever wear this one style. It's very kind of people to send them, but I don't think they'll get worn, unless I give them to my friends, though I do often give them to fans standing outside the gates at the studios.

The fans have been really, really amazing. It's so nice that they've supported me in the way they have. I've never had fans before, apart from my mum. I've been getting lovely fan mail and messages and even the odd present. And I've been sent loads of free clothes by shops, which I'm obviously really pleased about.

The week before the first live shows was pretty intense. Everyone was doing their best to make us feel as comfortable as possible, but nothing can prepare you for walking out on stage in front of that many people. I'd performed in front of crowds, but this was more about the 15 million people who were watching at home.

I was becoming more and more aware of the fact that I needed to open my eyes when I was singing. Brian Friedman was screaming at me in rehearsals, and he kept saying over and over that I had to learn to look up. It was just a confidence thing, and also the way I was used to singing when I was in pubs and clubs. Back then, people didn't care whether or not I was looking at them and it was fine for me to be in my own little world.

It was obviously a problem when it came to TV, though, because Dannii said it too: 'Share your performance, really connect, look at the audience and look down that camera.' I had to get the hang of it quickly if I didn't want people to think I was massively shy, which I'm not.

Walking out on stage for the first show was electric. Hearing the audience go mad and knowing that you're about to sing live for possibly the biggest audience you will ever sing for in your entire life is just incredible. All I could think was 'Please don't forget your words, whatever you do, and don't mess this up.' I looked at the red light on top of this camera and it was pointing directly at me and I thought, 'God, that's live telly.'

I sang David Guetta's 'When Love Takes Over' in Week 1, which is a great song. The idea came from Dannii and the producer Biff Stannard. I could let rip on it, which was cool. I don't think anything can compare to how I felt when I was performing it. It was inexplicably good.

That should have been the time when I looked back and remembered how I came to be there, but honestly it went so quickly that I forgot about everything else, including how many people were watching. I got lost in the song, but in a good way because I still remembered to look out at the audience and I had Brian's words going round in my head.

opposite page

The worst part of the show – Sunday nights, but Dannii helped me through

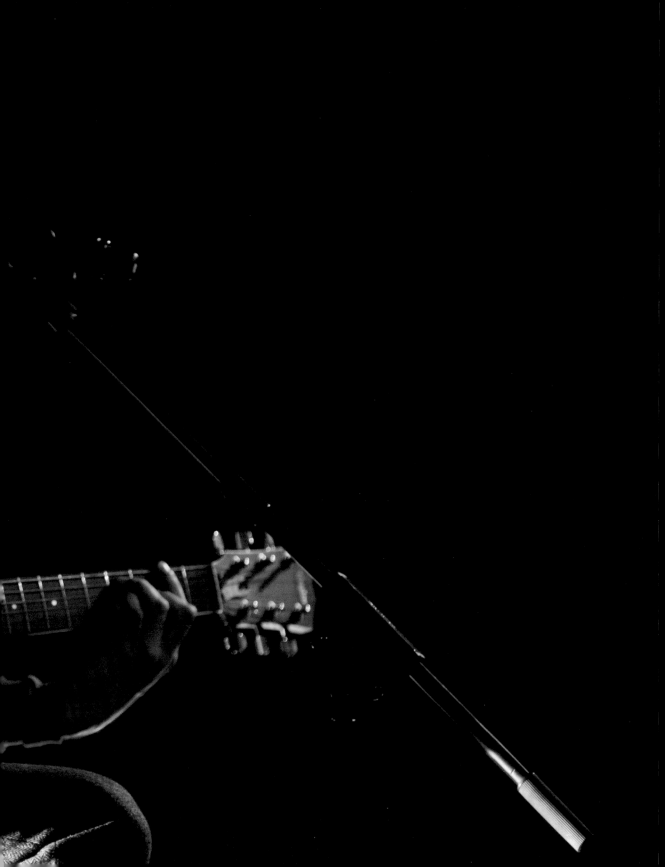

It was brilliant working with Brian during the competition and I've got so much respect for him. I think he's a genius and such a great guy to work with, so I've always listened to any advice he's given me.

My confidence got better and better as time went on because I was always improving, and that was down to all the things I was told by the singing teachers and producers and everyone else who helped me. I always had self-belief; I guess I just had a very different style of singing from some of the other contestants, so they had to bring out more of a TV performer in me.

'Louis told me I was in it for the long haul and described me as a "music man". I was so happy.'

I had no idea how the judges would react or what kind of comments they'd make after my first performance, so when Louis told me I was in it for the long haul and described me as a 'music man', I was so happy. Then Simon described my performance as 'genius' and I put my hands up to my face because I was so shocked. Simon also told me I needed to get some self-belief, and I could see where he was coming from, I guess. I know I came across as really shaky even though I tried my best not to.

I was worried about the Sunday night, of course, because someone had to go, and when I got through I was so chuffed. I was sad to see FYD and Nicolo go, because I don't think they got a fair chance, but I suppose that's the way it happens. I felt really relieved when I got back to the house, but it felt a little bit emptier with those six people gone, and it got more and more empty as the weeks went on.

previous pages

I definitely felt most comfortable when I had my guitar for support

opposite page

By now I was really starting to enjoy myself

Week 2

Before I knew it, we were gearing up for Week 2's live show. The previous Saturday had been insane. It was so scary, but at the same time it was one of the best nights of my life. It was just an incredible experience and I couldn't wait for this week so I could try to deal with the nerves a little bit better. I was definitely a bit wobbly in Week 1, but it was the first time round so I tried not to give myself a hard time about it.

I still couldn't get my head around people recognising me, which was happening more and more since the first live show. It had been happening for a while, but it's easy to forget about it when you're hanging out with everyone else in the competition, because everything somehow becomes normal. Then it's so odd when all of a sudden a pap starts chasing you down the street when you've popped out to the shop. It didn't feel real then, and it still doesn't now.

Someone told me in Week 2 that I'd already been named as the bookies' favourite, which put a bit more pressure on me, obviously. People were expecting me to be good because I was being talked about. It's not necessarily a positive thing to be the bookies' favourite at such an early stage. You just have to look at what happened to Danyl the previous year. One minute everyone was saying he was going to win, and the next he got voted off. Things happen and it goes up and down so quickly. All I could do was my level best each weekend, try my hardest to improve and maybe stay the favourite if I could.

The theme for Week 2 was Heroes, and I was singing Bruno Mars's 'Just the Way You Are', which is such a beautiful song and I really wanted to do it justice. I'd never actually heard the single before Tim Byrne, who is one of the Creative Directors, played it to me. As soon as I heard it I was like 'Love it, love it, love it.' I was attempting a high C during the song, which is a killer, but I decided that I could either play it safe or really go for it. And what do you gain if you don't take a risk?

I loved performing it and felt I'd done as good a job as I could. When Louis said it was note-perfect I was on such a high. Then he likened me to Bono, which felt absolutely ridiculous as I don't think I'm anything like him, but I knew he meant it as a compliment so of course I took it like that. Simon told me he thought I appeared nervous and that I fell off here and there, which is kind of what I thought anyway, and once again he mentioned my confidence. I did feel like it was growing week after week, though. I was definitely getting there.

I felt really bad for Diva Fever going home on the Sunday night. I don't think people took them seriously. As for Storm, I just don't think he was what people were looking for in the competition, but I think that vocally he was one of the best and he was so professional.

Needless to say, I learnt early on in the competition that Sundays were the hardest days. You have this massive high on the Saturday night, performing and seeing friends and family backstage, then come Sunday someone has to go and you've got all that time to wait until you find out who it is. Every week I knew it could be me, and it does make you feel unnerved. In a matter of hours you could go from living in this massive house and being watched by millions, to heading home and back to normal life.

I found it incredibly tough standing up on stage week after week, and of course so did everyone else. That moment when Dermot is announcing who's safe is so tense I can't even begin to describe it. We were all supportive of each other, though, which was nice.

Of course, everyone got on better with some people than with others, and I'm not going to pretend it was one big happy family all the time, because as you'd expect, there was bickering at times. We were in a high-pressure situation and people were sometimes stressed out and tired, but generally I think we were all there for each other and no one wanted to see any of the others go.

Week 3

We went on a shopping trip to Topshop in Week 3; it was all filmed and I found it quite terrifying. We were totally mobbed, and while I'm always happy to stop and chat to people, or to go out and meet anyone who's waiting outside if we're in the studio or whatever, this was completely different.

It was quite scary because the crowd was massive and it was almost impossible even to get into the shop. I felt bad because we were moved on so quickly that I didn't get a chance to stop and speak to anyone. That was one of the points when I realised how big everything had got with the show and that we'd all become 'faces', if you like. Not famous as such, but well known. Actually, recognisable is an even better term. I might accept the 'fame' title in a few years if I've managed to cement my career and have success, but for now I really don't deserve it. I would never want to call myself a celebrity, because I hate the word, but feeling genuinely famous one day would be pretty cool.

When I looked back at my Week 2 performance of 'Just the Way You Are' on TV afterwards I could see it was pretty wobbly in places. I think I got a bit over-excited half-way through and rushed the last part, which was a mistake. I knew that once I could conquer the nerves, I could really concentrate on coming out strong.

The entire competition was just so unbelievable. Every Saturday became the best Saturday I'd ever had in my life. To be praised by the judges and to get a good response felt like nothing else I'd ever experienced.

Every day I woke up in *The X Factor* house, I'd bounce out of bed because I knew that something amazing was going to happen. I'm quite lazy and would happily lie in bed all day if I was back at home, but here there was always something cool to do. Every day was different and exciting, and I wanted to enjoy it as much as I could because I never knew when it was going to end. Everything was a first – our first live performance, our first photo shoot and our first time in the studio. You never knew what you would be doing and when, and the whole thing was a huge buzz.

Being backstage every week was also a lot of fun. I enjoyed all the rehearsals and getting styled and hanging out with everyone before the show. There were times, though, when I needed to just go off somewhere and have a bit of time to myself because things were always quite manic. We didn't have changing rooms as such, we had trailers, and we'd end up getting ready in a corridor or somewhere, which was funny, and it wasn't always easy to find a quiet spot. But as long as I had five minutes to get myself together before I performed, I was happy.

In Week 3, I sang Britney Spears' 'Baby One More Time...' and if I'm being honest, I wasn't totally convinced it was going to work. It's one of those songs that is strongly associated with Britney and I really needed to put my own spin on it if I didn't want it to sound like a karaoke classic, which it is. I was desperate to make it credible, and Biff's production of the track was amazing, so I'm so grateful to him for that.

I loved that night, and the audience reaction I got was crazy. I felt so emotional and all I could do was clasp my hands together and say thank you. I felt really humbled. That was one of those light-bulb moments where I thought, 'You know what? They think I'm good. I am good.'

Cheryl said that listening to me was like being in an unplugged session, and Simon said he was glad I'd taken the risk because it had paid off. That spurred me on to want to take more risks if I was still in the competition the following week. I wanted to try everything.

As ever, after an amazing Saturday night, Sunday night inevitably followed and someone had to go. This week it was John and I shed a tear for him. I can honestly say he is one of the nicest guys I've ever met in or outside *The X Factor*. He's so talented and I don't think he got a real chance to prove himself on TV. I don't think people got to see the real John, which is this amazing guy.

I know it's a competition, and I knew I shouldn't have got emotionally involved, but it was hard because you became so close to people and all of a sudden they were gone. I missed him a hell of a lot.

Week 4

Although I got good feedback for my 'Baby One More Time...' performance and the crowd made me feel unbelievable, I had a bit of a confidence crisis a few days later. You can't be good all the time, so I was waiting for the moment when the judges would say, 'You know what? It wasn't all that good.' Every week after my performance I couldn't help saying to myself, 'You could have done better,' even though I knew it was counter-productive.

The theme for Week 4 was Halloween, and the track I was singing, Leona Lewis's 'Bleeding Love', is such a big song that I felt I had a lot to live up to. Brian said to me it was 'One of those songs that you don't touch,' and Simon joked, 'Not many people can pull this off, and I've heard some horrific attempts over the years. Best of luck!' Those comments made me ask myself whether I'd made the right decision, and I did have a last-minute freak-out wondering if I should choose a different track.

It was another risk that I was willing to take, but this one didn't quite come off. The judges' comments weren't dreadful, but they weren't great, and it was definitely my worst week so far by a country mile. Cheryl said I looked a bit defeated as soon as I walked out, and maybe she was right. Perhaps I was more nervous than I realised.

I think at the back of my mind I was worried that everyone would compare me to Leona, because her version is so incredible. I didn't want to give a bad performance that week of all weeks because of Leona's history with the show, and I think I almost told myself it wouldn't work before I'd even tried. But you live and learn.

I was in a bad headspace generally that week. There was a lot of stuff coming out in the papers about me and I found the press attention hard to handle. I tried to ignore anything bad that was written or to take it with a pinch of salt, but to go from being completely unknown to having things said about you in the papers every day is quite hard to get

your head around. I was most upset when people I knew sold stories or photos. Someone stole a picture of me from my friend's Facebook page and sold it, and that really, really annoyed me.

To think that people I trusted were betraying me was a hard thing to swallow, but at the end of the day I'm not stupid and of course I knew that there would be some level of press attention that comes with being in *The X Factor* – it's the biggest show in the country. I really did just try and get on with it and not worry too much, especially when things were written that weren't true. There's nothing you can do about it, so there's no point in getting stressed.

I got linked with a lot of women during the show, like Grace, the stylist. It was all rumours though. Just because you get on with someone, the next minute, you're apparently in love. It's a bit frustrating, but you just have to get on with it and not worry about it.

I thought I would definitely be in the bottom two come Sunday night, and would probably go after my not-so-great performance, but people voted to keep me in, which was amazing and I still can't thank them enough. Belle Amie went in the end, which was a shame as they were good I thought, and they were sweet girls, but they had a good run. Traditionally, bands don't do that well in *The X Factor*, especially girl bands, so they did really well to get as far as they did. I also thought it was such a shame to see Katie in the bottom two again. I know she got a lot of stick in the press, but it was incredible the way she kept everything together. I have a lot of respect for that.

Week 5

I felt so angry with myself when I looked back on the previous week's performance. I felt like I'd let myself down. But stuff happens and you just have to get up and do it all again and try to be better. In terms of preparing for the show, the important thing for me was to have some time

to myself before I went on stage, to get my head together. I didn't really have a pre-performance ritual as such. Every week I just concentrated on singing well, remembering my words and hoping I would be fine. Having said that, I did wear my lucky green socks every week. I didn't even wash them in-between, so they did smell slightly by the end. Luckily Grace didn't try and put me in three-quarter-length trousers at any point – we would probably have fallen out because I would still have tried to wear my green socks. It would have been a bit of an issue.

I'd sung mainly women's songs during the competition up until that point. In fact, I'd only sung one guys' song in my entire experience on *The X Factor*, and that was 'Just the Way You Are'. What can I say? I guess I'm just a big girl myself. Actually, it's really more that women's songs seem to suit the tone of my voice and I enjoy singing them, and I don't think that's a bad thing.

I decided to sing another woman's song in Week 5, Roberta Flack's 'The First Time (Ever I Saw Your Face)'. As I've already explained, it's a song that means an incredible amount to me and I was quite surprised they let me perform it, as I wasn't sure it was very *X Factor*. I didn't feel stressed about singing it, because I love the track so much. At the same time, because it's so dear to me, I wanted to make it sound the very best that I could.

Getting a standing ovation from the judges was so overwhelming. And that, mixed with how emotional I was already feeling, meant that I couldn't help starting to well up. It was hard breaking down live on TV in front of so many people, because I didn't want to look like a pansy and not many people knew the story and what the song meant to me. But if I hadn't let it all out, I probably would have exploded. I felt completely overwhelmed and I was in tears backstage afterwards.

My family were there to watch me and I think they shed a little tear as well. I was just so happy that I didn't totally mess it up.

I was really hoping that I'd done enough on the Saturday to get through again on Sunday, and I was so happy once again that people voted for me. TreyC went, which was a bit of a shock as she had such a great voice.

Week 6

The Pride of Britain awards, which we all went to in Week 6, was such a great event to be at and a real honour. I got to meet some really inspirational people and I felt very humbled to meet some of the soldiers and kids who have been through so much. I also met some sports stars like Joe Calzaghe and Jermain Defoe, and it was mad because some of the celebrities were coming over to our table to say hello to us. I don't get starstruck, but it is nice to meet people and find out what they're like first hand.

We also went to the premiere of *Harry Potter and the Deathly Hallows* in London's Leicester Square, and I honestly never thought that I would be walking down a red carpet like that. It was an incredible night, but I didn't feel like I deserved to be there. Then for some of the cast to turn round and recognise me and say that they liked what I was doing was just wicked. We met Daniel Radcliffe and he was such a sweet guy and very quietly told me I was his favourite. He also got me to speak to his girlfriend on the phone, which was very sweet.

this page

Despite all the perks, I still felt like just a normal lad

Helena Bonham Carter also told me she liked me, and I was absolutely speechless. She's a legend. Then she came to the studio to see the show a couple of weeks later and we had a chat. She's properly amazing, so it was a bit surreal standing there talking to her. As I say, I don't really get starstruck, but I'll happily admit that I did when I met *her*. She had a big effect on me.

As the weeks went on, I realised more and more how lucky we boys were to have Dannii as our mentor. She's such a busy lady but she still had plenty of time for us. She was always on the other end of the phone when we needed her, and she was in the studio with us being hands-on. She did such a wonderful job and it was reflected in the fact that the boys kept getting through every Sunday. That had a lot do with how much Dannii and her team did for us.

Dannii and I decided to push things a bit further for Week 6 with a song that even she admitted was 'vocal gymnastics' – Elton John's 'Goodbye Yellow Brick Road'. I wasn't a huge fan of the song and I'm not even a big Elton John fan, but I decided to just do my best and have fun with it. I absolutely couldn't afford to drop my game, so I had to go out there and really give it 100 per cent, especially after the reaction I'd received the previous week.

When Simon said he'd happily have listened to more, and Dannii said, 'Whether I was in a stadium watching you, or a private little gig, I felt like you were singing that to me,' I couldn't have asked for better comments.

I was in total shock when Aiden went on the Sunday night. I thought it was a bad, bad decision. He is so talented. He and I had been through everything together. We weren't leaning on each other as such, but we were friends right from Bootcamp to the live shows. We had each other's back. We slept in the same room, ate together, got in taxis together. He's like my brother so it was always going to be a blow if he went.

We spoke about it afterwards and it was really hard to see him go. It was weird from the first moment he went. The house felt much quieter because we'd spent so much time together, but we'll definitely be mates for life.

Week 7

Despite not really expecting to, I very much enjoyed singing 'Goodbye Yellow Brick Road'. The week before had been pretty serious so I wanted to have a bit more of a laugh on stage, and I think I did that. I was the first

to perform in Week 7, which is always a bit scary. Aiden leaving proved to me how unpredictable the competition could be and that no one was safe, and seeing him go gave me the kick up the arse that I needed to spur me on. It made me want to win it more than ever.

Our group song this week was 'Heroes', which we recorded for the charity Help For Heroes. It was such a pleasure to be involved with it and a privilege to go down to Headley Court in Surrey and meet the injured soldiers. The charity has only been going for three years and it should have been going for much longer than that. It was so nice to be involved in the single. It really is an absolute honour. Watching the VT of Matthew Wilson before the show really brought it home to me just how much all the soldiers do for our country. I nearly started crying as soon as I saw him, and it was brilliant that he wanted to come down to the show.

This was, without a doubt, my favourite group song. I've kind of enjoyed them all, but Aiden and I used to joke that we dreaded them each week, and then when the doors opened we were like, 'Sod it, let's go and have a laugh.' Some of them were a bit cheesy, but also fun. You've just got to throw yourself into everything or you end up looking even more stupid.

In The Beatles week I sang 'Come Together', but I overcooked the vocal in a big way. I forgot about the extra 10 per cent you give it when you're actually doing it live and the adrenaline that comes from being on stage, so I lashed it up and was really annoyed with myself afterwards. It sounded fine in sound-check but I kept pushing it and everything went a bit Noddy Holder. If I could erase that performance from iTunes and YouTube, I would. It's just horrendous when I look back on it, and it's definitely one of those moments that I hope will be forgotten in time.

The vest I wore on stage that week seemed to get a lot of attention, but I didn't actually mean to wear it. It reached the point where I was due to perform and still no one could decide what I was going to wear over the vest, so in the end I threw off the shirt and jacket I was wearing at the time and walked out on stage.

opposite page

The Help For Heroes single was such a worthy cause to be involved with

As I said, I always like to have five minutes' downtime to get ready before I go on stage. Not in a diva way, but just so I can relax and not be pulled and poked around. Just seconds before I was due to start, we were still messing about with what I was going to wear, and I wasn't happy, so off everything came.

'The vest I wore on stage that week seemed to get a lot of attention, but I didn't actually mean to wear it.'

When I walked on stage I shrugged at Dannii and she just kind of shrugged back at me, but I could tell Simon was thinking, 'What the hell is he wearing?' I was so stressed out by that point that I didn't even care. In fact I felt comfortable just wearing a vest. Some people seemed to really like it and some people thought I looked a bit trailer-trash, but whatever. Dannii said afterwards it was probably a good move because a lot of women had been Tweeting about it, but it honestly wasn't intentional.

For the first time ever, I had dancers on stage with me, which was great. I suppose it gave me a bit more of a swagger, rather than if it had just been me standing at a mic stand going 'eeeeee'. The dancers were a little bit distracting but very nice. I'm not really one of those people who wants to put on a big performance or wander around the stage like the big 'I am', but it was good to do something different.

If I was given the choice, I would sit with my guitar each week and just sing, but it is a TV show and people want to be entertained, so I can understand why things need to be a bit more visual sometimes.

I got mixed comments from the judges. Simon said that, thanks to the vest, I looked like I'd just been dragged from the loo, but he did praise

my vocals; Louis said he felt there was something missing, but Cheryl said she was really enjoyed it and that it was nice to see the cheeky chappie coming out in me.

Although we always used to joke with each other during Saturday's rehearsals about who would be going home the following evening, when the time came, it wasn't a laughing matter at all, and we were all as nervous and scared about leaving as each other.

It was Paije who went that Sunday. I was gutted to see him go, because he was a brilliant guy with a great voice. He was also the last of the boys apart from me. But, on a selfish level, it meant I then had Dannii to myself.

Week 8

I was very careful not to make the same mistake two weeks in a row. I was not going to overdo my vocal and mess it up again. For the first time, we each sang two songs, which was hard-going, and of course it was the chance to qualify for the all-important semi-final the following weekend. The past eight weeks had completely flown by and I couldn't believe we were almost on the home stretch.

My bedroom in the house became a lot tidier now that I was completely on my own. I was pretty tidy generally, but when you know someone is going to come in and throw clothes on the floor you tend not to bother too much. One Direction's bedroom was without a doubt the messiest. You could barely see the floor and sometimes couldn't even open the door. What do you expect with five teenage boys? I was just happy I wasn't sharing with them!

My first song on Week 8's live show was 'I Love Rock'n'Roll', and although the judges gave me good feedback I didn't think I deserved it, as it wasn't my best performance by a long shot. The dancers were incredible but it didn't feel very 'me'.

I loved having my guitar on stage with me again for the second song, 'Nights in White Satin'. It's such an amazing track. Cheryl said it was my best performance ever, Simon said it was one of the best versions of the song he'd ever heard, and Louis called it emotional and heart-wrenching. I was so touched by all of those comments and hoped the public liked it as much and would vote for me.

I was so nervous on the Sunday, especially as it was a double eviction. When Dermot said my name, I was so shocked and couldn't get my head around the fact that I was going to be in the semi-finals. I won't say I cried about Wagner going, because everyone knows we've had our differences, but I do wish him the best of luck. And Katie too. Whatever she decides to do, I hope it's a success.

We had some more brilliant celebrity guests in Week 8, and throughout the whole competition. I thought Nicole Scherzinger was incredible. Other favourites of mine over the weeks were Katy Perry, Take That, Westlife and Bon Jovi.

I had a really good talk with Robbie backstage when Take That were on. He wanted to have a chat to me about all the things that were coming out in the press about me, and it was really sweet of him to take time out and talk to me about it.

He was really helpful too. He said, 'I've been in the business for 20 years and it still hurts when things come out in the papers about me.' It was great for me, because I did get a lot of flak for whatever reason, but he just said to keep my head held high and get on with doing my job. He also said, 'There will be people out there who won't like what you do, but also a lot of people who will like what you do. So ignore the bad and concentrate on the good.' They were good words of encouragement.

BECOMING A
STAR

The Semi-final

We went to the *Narnia* premiere in Week 9, so we were on the red carpet again. It felt weird going to events like that because we were still just contestants on a TV show, but it was snowing and we also got to see the fans and have our photos taken with them, so it was great.

This week we also each got to film the winner's video, which was an amazing experience. We'd already appeared in the 'Heroes' video, but this was very different as there weren't loads of other people backing you up on this one – it was just me, on my own, so there was much more pressure. We filmed it in a studio in East London. It had snowed loads the night before and I was slightly worried that we'd never be able to get there, but in the end it was fine.

I got to wear a nice suit and some cool shoes – which Grace had been trying to make me wear for a while – and I really, really enjoyed it, despite not feeling 100 per cent. I'd been feeling rough for a couple of days and it really kicked in that day. It was like flu but mainly on my chest. It was not fun.

I started to feel more and more ill as Week 9 went on, which was a total disaster. There was a question mark over whether I'd even be able

to sing on the Saturday night. I had to miss rehearsals on the Friday so that I could stay in bed and try to get better for the live show. It was a nightmare. Of all the weeks for this to happen, it had to be semi-final week, which is just so important.

Come Saturday night, I was feeling worse than ever and I was very concerned about my performances. 'You've Got The Love' was without a doubt a bit of a struggle, and I didn't do anywhere near as well as I wanted to. But I tried my best and, all things considered, I did okay.

'I was also worried that it would be my last ever performance on *The X Factor*, and I didn't want to leave having not sung my best.'

Simon said my second performance of 'She's Always a Woman' was one of my worst on the series and I completely agree with him; it wasn't what I wanted it to be. I'd wanted to do a ballad, something that I could really put my heart into, and it felt very frustrating not to be able to give it everything I've got. My voice just wasn't up to it that night.

I was also worried that it would be my last ever performance on *The X Factor*, and I didn't want to leave having not sung my best. Thankfully, the other judges said some really nice things about both songs. I think it was pretty obvious from how I looked that I was ill but still trying to do everything I could.

I was both shocked and relieved to stay in on the Sunday night. I was sad to see Mary go, but I would have been sad to see anyone go because we had all become so close. I could not get my head around the fact that I

opposite page

Filming the winner's single

following pages

Backstage after the semi-final the atmosphere was electric. I felt like a winner just being there

FPS **25.000**   SHUTTER **180.0**   EI **800**   WB **3200** CC **+0**

●STBY   SxS 1 **12MIN**

BAT 1 **23.2 V**

was in the final, and I was so grateful to everyone who had voted to keep me in, even though it was far from my best performance of the series. Thank you everyone; it meant the world to me. I was just praying that I'd feel better in time for the final so that I could come back and give the best performance of my life.

The Final

I could not believe I'd made it all the way to the final! I'd been so worried the previous week with my voice not being up to scratch, so to know that I was in the last four and had a genuine shot at winning felt insane. I'd been struggling with illness again all week, but I'd done everything I could to get better. Obviously I needed to put in extra rehearsals to prepare for the weekend, but I also made sure that I got loads of rest.

The home visit was one of the biggest highlights of the competition for me. Going back to my local pub in Colchester to perform was brilliant as I got to see so many people I hadn't seen for a while, and it felt good to be back to normality after the craziness of the last few months. Not that it was exactly normal there; the whole place was packed and people were hanging out of windows and all sorts. I can't describe how great that felt.

I got to have a pint and then I performed for everyone, and while I was singing everything just hit me and I started crying. Just seeing all the support I was getting blew me away and I got a bit overwhelmed.

The next stop was my parents' house. Dannii came along as well and I loved getting to introduce her to everyone. We had some champagne and I thanked my parents for everything they've done for me and for being there every step of the way. It was very emotional and when my dad told me he'd never given up on me I got upset again. Then my dad and I had a moment in the kitchen when we were chatting and we both got teary again and had a massive hug. I don't think I've ever cried so much in one day, but it was all happy crying.

opposite page

Walking off after performing 'Here With Me'. My head was spinning!

135

Later on that day I played a big local gig and it was absolutely nuts. There were fireworks and huge crowds – police were there to control them. To walk out to that amount of people was amazing. That's the reason I'm doing this. To think how quickly this has all taken off is just crazy.

We kicked off the live show on the Saturday night by singing 'What a Feeling' for our group song. It was great to see the other contestants back, like Aiden and Belle Amie. I was so nervous before going on stage, even for that. All the finalists were. It was a big deal.

Then it was time for my first song, and I did Dido's 'Here With Me', which is a great track. I was still a bit worried about my voice, but it went well, thankfully. Afterwards Louis said I deserved to be in the final, Cheryl said she knew I'd be there and Simon said he hoped I'd still be there on the Sunday. That all felt incredible, but what made me feel happiest of all was when Dannii thanked for me for working so hard. She's been so fantastic throughout the competition and I want to do her proud.

'My second song of the night was "Unfaithful", and to me duetting with Rihanna was almost beyond belief.'

My second song of the night was 'Unfaithful', and to me duetting with Rihanna was almost beyond belief. I am a genuine fan, I think she's amazing. Even as I was introducing her I was still in shock. It was a moment I'll never forget. She was incredible and it was one of the best nights of my life.

As soon as I woke up on the Sunday it hit me that it was the finals. I was still feeling really ill and I had to go to the doctor on the Sunday morning to have my vocal chords looked at, just to make sure that they were okay and I wasn't going to do them any permanent damage by singing that night. Thankfully they gave me the all clear and said I'd be all right, but I knew I was going to struggle a little bit.

From the doctors I went straight to rehearsals, which didn't go as well as they could have done because of my throat. I was so frustrated that I wasn't well. I did manage to get through a decent version of my winner's single 'When We Collide' – a cover of a Biffy Clyro song – thank goodness. It's such a great song and to do a bad version would have gutted me, so I then felt I'd be all right for the evening.

Performing with Take That at the beginning of the show was just such an amazing way to kick it off. What can I say? It was such a good moment.

Again, I was worried about my voice, but Dannii had said to me that I just had to go on and do my best – that's all I could do. If I thought about the fact that it was the grand final, she said, it would make me even more nervous and might affect my voice more too, so I just had to put that out of my head. I had to go out and treat this like any other Sunday night, which wasn't the easiest thing I've ever done.

I should have done my performance of 'Firework' a lot better than I did but, again, my throat let me down. Everyone said they enjoyed it, but I didn't think it was my best performance. I'm a perfectionist so I always feel I could have done better. What I say to myself is that if you strive for perfection you may not achieve it, but you will constantly improve.

Because my performances weren't as good as I wanted them to be, when I was standing on stage with One Direction and Rebecca for the first cut I had no idea whether or not I would be going through to the final two. I thought everyone worked their socks off that night to give it everything, so it was impossible to call it.

opposite page

I can't believe my luck!

My throat could have ruined it for me, so when my name was called out and I was through I felt like my head was going to explode. I was in the final two, and I can't even describe how brilliant that felt. I felt so, so lucky.

The next hour was terrifying, but it seemed to fly by because there was so much going on around me. I don't think there was one second where I was standing still on my own, which was good as it kept my mind occupied.

When it was down to Rebecca and me and we were both standing on stage looking at each other, everything seemed to go a bit fuzzy and I thought my legs were going to give way underneath me.

Being there on stage with Dannii, waiting to hear if I had won, was one of the most nerve-wracking experiences of my life. Then, when Dermot called my name out and I knew I'd won, it was like a bomb had gone off. My ears started ringing and I just remember hugging Dannii and then looking out into the crowd and seeing everyone clapping.

Rebecca was so gracious to me and came over and hugged me and said congratulations. I have no doubt that she's going to do some amazing things in the future. She's so talented.

I was so grateful when all of the contestants came on stage when I was singing 'When We Collide' again, because I honestly wasn't sure that I'd get through it. I was failing that time around, because my voice was finally giving up on me. I think I'd put it through quite enough.

Everyone watching on TV saw me hitting Dannii in the face with my mic as well, which I feel awful about. Things were so hectic and I was being pulled all over the place so I could barely see in front of me. I did text her to apologise the following day, and I hope she forgives me.

I'm still in a complete daze about winning and I have been ever since that second when Dermot said my name. I'm in massive shock. I was so nervous all weekend, and now that's lifted and it's all over it feels amazing. All the other acts were so lovely congratulating me. Everyone seemed to be really happy for me.

Afterwards I just hugged my friends and family and I thought my dad would explode he was so happy. I really felt like I'd done it for my family as much as myself.

I would love to say that I then went and partied to celebrate that night, but I actually went back to the contestants' house and ate some cold chicken nuggets from the night before, and then went to sleep.

'I think *The X Factor* really pushed the boundaries this year with the people they had on the show and I've loved being a part of it.'

I still wasn't feeling 100 per cent and I didn't want to drink any alcohol. There's plenty of time for partying and you can bet that as soon as I get a chance I'll be out there. But I'm also looking forward to going back home to my local and spending time with my friends and being as normal as I possibly can be.

I also need to clean out my bag, which I know sounds a bit odd. I'm quite superstitious, and I decided that if I got through a round I wouldn't take anything out of it, so it's filled with rubbish and sweet wrappers. Now it's all over I think I need to get rid of all that stuff and start over.

I think *The X Factor* really pushed the boundaries this year with the people they had on the show, and I've loved being a part of it. Being on the show has changed me in a few ways too. I've grown thicker skin and I take things with a pinch of salt, which I didn't do so much before.

I'm also a slightly more grown-up person than I was when I first went into the competition, in a really good way. I'm still a big kid, but I've learnt to talk to people in a better way because I've had to learn to think on my feet and watch what comes out of my mouth ... I think before I speak now, so it's taught me new skills in that way.

I don't think I've changed who I am, though. I was totally myself throughout the whole competition and I plan to carry on being like that. I'm 27 and I know who I am and how I am now, so it's not like I'm a teenager who is still developing a personality. I take my hat off to the likes of One Direction and Cher, who are much younger but still dealt with all the attention very well. I think we all just took every week as it came and dealt with it as best we could.

The worst bits of the past six months have been the waiting around and the stressing out and not knowing what's going on, so it's a relief that's all over and I can sit back and enjoy it.

Also, being ill was obviously awful so I plan to do a lot of sleeping and look after myself before the hard work kicks in again. Things are going to be pretty busy from now on, but it's going to feel weird going back to living in my normal house without cameras on me all the time.

this page

Rebecca and I prepare to face the results. She looked stunning that night

The best bits of the entire competition for me were getting to perform every single Saturday night, especially performing with Rihanna. She is so amazing and people said it was a sexy performance, and I think it was. I also loved singing 'Nights in White Satin' and 'The First Time (Ever I Saw Your Face)'. Those two songs were standouts for me.

Another thing I loved was getting to spend time with Dannii, Cheryl, Simon and Louis. They were all so supportive and it was a total pleasure getting to know them all.

And of course I'm so happy that I won it for team Dannii and the boys. I wanted to justify the faith she had in putting me through when we were in Australia. It seems so long ago now that we were there, but at the same time the memories are still completely clear in my mind.

The Future

I don't think everything has sunk in yet. I think that once I look back on the show I'll realise just how much we've done. It's all been such a whirlwind that we honestly haven't had time to sit down and think about it too much.

I know I'll be staying in touch with a lot of people from the show, especially Aiden and Dannii. I met so many amazing people during my time on the show, and I feel I've made some genuine, lifelong friends. I think we're all going to carry on supporting each other and I wish all of them the best of luck.

One thing I am going to have to get used to, which I still haven't, is all the press attention. I heard so many funny rumours about myself. The best one was that I went out for dinner with Simon Cowell and he made me pay, which never happened. There was also stuff about me and Grace the stylist that wasn't true, and things about me and some of the dancers which had no basis whatsoever.

It's all been a bit crazy, so I've just tried my best to keep my nose out of it and not get involved or even listen to it too much, otherwise it could have really started to bother me. As long as I know the truth, and my friends and family know the truth, that's the important thing.

I think I am going to have to be a bit more careful with people in the future. I'm very aware of the reasons why people are giving me attention. I've got more friends than I've ever had in my life now, but I know who my real friends are.

I don't want to sound horribly cynical, but I am a very trusting person. I like people in general and I try to see the good in everyone, so I need to look after myself. I know that some people are just out to make money or whatever, so sometimes you need to be a bit wary.

As far as women go, of course if I meet someone and fall madly in love, then great, but I am single at the moment and I'm fine with that. The thing about being in the public eye is that you sit down and have

opposite page

I'm trying to sing after I'd been told I'd won. I don't think I've ever been happier

breakfast with someone and all of a sudden you're apparently madly in love. It's so funny.

I've got so many ideas about what I'd like to do music wise in the future. I would love to work with a band because I love that feeling of camaraderie and having a team around you. There's nothing better than having that shared experience and buzzing around with people. I would also love to be heavily involved in the songwriting side. I've been writing since I was 11 and it's something I plan to continue with and incorporate into whatever I do.

It still feels surreal that I've released my own single, and to think that I'll soon be starting work on an album is just mind-blowing. It's what I've wanted to do all my life, and now it's finally happening. I want to make this album and be heavily involved in the future of it and have a long and successful career. I want to do big things and do all of the things that come with being a musician.

I've got masses of ideas and I want to make all of the people who supported me proud. I would love to do loads of gigs in the future because singing live is what I'm all about. Singing in front of a crowd – no matter how big or small – is where I'm happiest.

Thank you once again for all your support and here's to a hell of a lot of fun in the future!

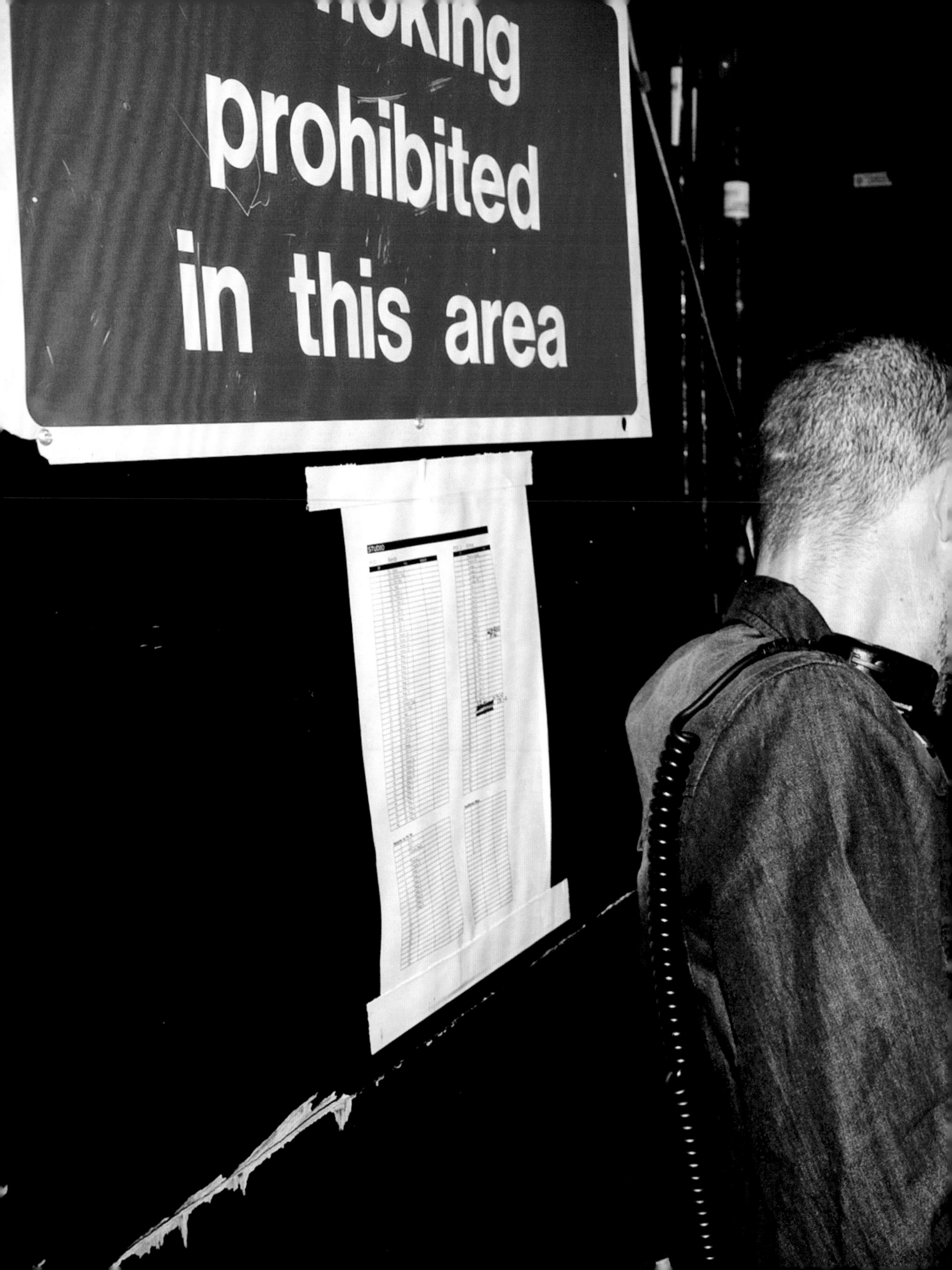
prohibited
in this area

PASSES 04/12/10

WHITE - CONTESTANT PA

PURPLE PASS WITH PURPL
X FACTOR CREW
ACCESS ALL AREAS

ORANGE PASS WITH PURPL
FACTOR
ACCESS ALL AREAS

PINK STRIPE PASS WITH PI
SUPPORTING
STUDIO
DAY ONLY

BLACK
STUDIO
DAY ONLY

Restaurant

ACCESS A

X FACTOR PASS - CHA
STUDIO RESTAURANT IN DAY

Thanks

I'd like to thank my mum, my dad, my brothers and sisters, my dog Stella and all my family and friends.

Dannii Minogue, Nathan Smith, Biff, Savan Kotecha, Ali Bah Bah, Tyler Brown and Tim Byrne.

Simon Cowell, Louis Walsh, Cheryl Cole, Brian Friedman, Sisco and Tiana.

All the researchers – Rob Davies, Katie Hobbs, Joe Street, Helen Banoha, Josh Jacobs, Claire Bradley, Rebecca Morris, Kerry Plant and Dawn.

Everybody at Talkback, SYCO, Modest! and HarperCollins.

Alexi and all at Lee & Thompson.

Thanks to everyone at Fountain Studios – Tosh and all the security, Gabriel and all the crew. Tony and all the security staff at the house. Everyone at Sainsbury's. Liz and the make-up team, Adam and Paul and the hair team, Grace and the styling team and Alyson the spray lady. Dermot and Konnie. Polly and the press team.

Everybody who believed in me, Darren and Caroline Lingley and everybody at the Five Bells, Chris Heap, everybody at High Barn, all my Cunnys at the G Range. Adrian Marple, Phil and Bigitta, Andy Brown, Mr Donald, Damo Stone for all your help at Escape, John and everybody at the Swan and Bures, Jurga and Mark.

To anyone I may have forgotten – I apologise!
(This was done in a hurry!)

Simon Harris

Simon Harris is a renowned fashion photographer who regularly shoots editorial pieces for prestigious magazines, including *ID*, *Grazia*, *Drama*, *POP*, *Arena Homme Plus*, *Attitude*, *Perfect*, *Arise*, *Sunday Times Style* and *The Times*.

Simon also photographs for international fashion designers, such as Vivienne Westwood, Christopher Kane and Issa.

A long-standing member of *The X Factor* family, Simon has shot albums, singles and editorial campaigns for Olly Murs, Shayne Ward, Alexandra Burke, Jedward and Joe McElderry.

'It was an incredible experience working on *The X Factor* winner's book,' says Simon. 'I'm a massive fan of the show – it draws every emotion from the viewers and the artists both onstage and off. To be immersed in the bubble of *The X Factor* for so many months has been a privilege and a rollercoaster experience. For the book, I wanted to capture the excitement, drama and emotion as well as all those intimate moments that are so fascinating and make the show what it is. I hope this book gives readers a further glimpse into the world of *The X Factor* and the amazing people who make it happen.'

HarperCollins*Publishers*
77–85 Fulham Palace Road,
Hammersmith, London W6 8JB

www.harpercollins.co.uk

First published by HarperCollins*Publishers* 2010

10 9 8 7 6 5 4 3 2 1

Matt Cardle is represented exclusively by Richard Griffiths and
Harry Magee for Modest! Management.

The X Factor is a trademark of FremantleMedia Ltd and Simco Ltd.
Licensed by FremantleMedia Enterprises www.fremantlemedia.com

Principle photography © Simon Harris.
Images on pp 8/9, 14/15, 25, 26, 29, 30, 31, 32, 36, 40, 52, 54, 55, 63,
66, 68, 70/71, 74, 80, 81, 82/83, 87, 88, 90, 105, 114, 149, 150, 151, 155,
166, 185, 188, 202, 204/205, 219, 222 © FremantleMedia Ltd and Syco.
Special thank you to Ken McKay for the support photography.
Personal photographs on pp 16, 19, 20, 23 courtesy of the author.

A catalogue record of this book is available from the British Library

ISBN 978-0-00-742670-6

Printed and bound in Great Britain by Butler Tanner and Dennis Ltd,
Frome, Somerset

Mixed Sources
Product group from well-managed
forests and other controlled sources
www.fsc.org Cert no. TT-COC-2139
© 1996 Forest Stewardship Council